SCHOOL FOR CLOWNS, commissioned and first staged by the Unicorn Theatre, is one of the best new children's plays of the last few years. The basic idea is beautiful in its simplicity. On stage is a classroom with four pupils and one master. But the 'pupils' are apprentice clowns and the 'master' a grotesque demagogue whose job it is to instil in his charges the basic technique of clowning. So, the 'lessons' consist of the master reading out short scenarios which the clowns have to enact. Each of the sketches gets subtly out of hand as the master becomes involuntarily involved in the increasingly farcical proceedings . . .
'The pleasure,' wrote Michael Billington in *The* [illegible] 'lies in the battle between *their* anarchic indiv[illegible] discipline and in the class's inv[illegible] .'

With a cast of six alt[illegible] for small theatre groups in se[illegible] depends less on dialogue than [illegible] irector. The set is minimal, a[illegible] entiveness with which the ca[illegible] al of the situations. For this rea[illegible] to drama teachers in need of material in w[illegible] creativity is more important than verbal dexterity.

Age range: for audiences of 7-12 upwards.

'At last a children's show that is both inventive and original . . .'
The Guardian

'. . . One of the funniest children's shows, which, with its extraordinary visual quality, is just as much a treat for adults as children.'
Time Out

Other titles in the Theatre Box series include:

Death Angel	Brian Glover
Marmalade Atkins in Space	Andrew Davies
Reasons to be Cheerful	James Andrew Hall
The Prince and the Demons	George Moore
You Must Believe All This	Adrian Mitchell

SCHOOL FOR CLOWNS

A Play by F. K. Waechter
Translated by
Ken Campbell
With Cartoons by the Author

METHUEN · LONDON

A METHUEN PAPERBACK

First published in Great Britain in 1977 by Eyre Methuen Ltd, 11 New Fetter Lane, London EC4P 4EE
Reprinted 1980
Reprinted 1982 by Methuen London Ltd

Originally published in German under the title *Schule mit Clowns* by Friedrich Karl Waechter as the fourth volume in the series '3 mal Kindertheater'

ISBN 0 413 37650 8

Printed in Great Britain by Expression Printers Ltd, London

AUTHOR'S NOTE

I see two dangers for *School for Clowns* in performance. The first is that the play can drift too close to Will Hay and St Trinian's, with pupils hatching up merry japes to play on ossified pedagogues. The second is that the play might be seen as offering opportunities only for formal 'artistic clowning' too removed from the school situation. The clowns are alienated schoolchildren. Their characters ought to be drawn from that area rather than from traditional clownery. These pupils have the advantage over real schoolchildren in that they are better able to live out their fantasies by means of clowning. Similarly, the teacher is an alienated, present-day teacher who has to stick to the syllabus and must therefore demand discipline and curb fantasy.

The 'Chapters' were partly written for the five actors in the Frankfurt production and for their particular abilities. Which means that, if you can't perform adequately on the violin or the saxophone, the roller skates or the motorbike, then substitute other equally impressive activities.

F. K. Waechter
10 October 1976

TRANSLATOR'S NOTE

Big fun guaranteed!

School for Clowns
was first performed in English by the Unicorn Theatre Company at the Arts Theatre Club, London on 13 December 1975.
The cast was as follows:

WEASEL	Sylveste McCoy
PUFF	Chris Langham
PIMPLE	Matyelok Gibbs
DRIPPENS	Andy Andrews
PROFESSOR MOLEREASONS	Ken Campbell
MR BOGWORTH	Duncan Faber

Music composed and played by Ilona Sekacz

The play directed by Nicholas Barter

Designed by Anna Steiner

The scene throughout is a classroom

Schule mit Clowns

was first performed in German at the Schauspiel, Frankfurt-am-Main on 1 June 1975.

The four clowns were played by Wilfried Elste, Heinz Krähkamp, Ingo Lampe and Barbara Sukowa. Michael Altmann played the Professor.

The play was directed by Hermann Treusch and designed by Christian Steioff.

Act One

The curtain rises and we're in a classroom. Apart from a large, old-fashioned teacher's desk the room is bare of furniture. A cupboard, out of which will come many wonders, is built into one of the walls. There are three doors which I'll refer to as Door L., Door R., and Door C. Door C. is an important-looking double door, WEASEL *the Clown enters from Door R.* WEASEL *looks around.* WEASEL *tip-toes-cum-creeps to Door L., opens it and looks up the corridotr. No one there.* WEASEL *tip-toes-cum-creeps to important-looking double Door C., opens it, looks out. No one there.* WEASEL *closes door.*

WEASEL: Everybody's late. Or am I early? No one's here yet. Someone is here. I can see his feet. O it's me.

WEASEL *sits on the floor with his legs out straight, waiting to see if lessons begin. They don't. He gets up. He shuffles about. He converts his shuffle into a little dance. He finds some chalk on the teacher's desk. He smokes the chalk. He puts the chalk in his pocket. He finds a balloon in his pocket. He tries to pull it out. But it seems to be caught round his leg. As he tries to pull out the balloon, his leg jerks rhythmically like a marionette's. Eventually the balloon snaps free.*

Ouch!

WEASEL *blows his balloon up. He allows a bit of air to escape from the pinched nozzle of the balloon. The strange noise startles him. But he soon makes friends with it. The balloon escapes from his hand. He studies the balloon's flight through the air. He finds another balloon in his pocket. It too is caught round his leg. Previous episode repeated.*

Ouch!

WEASEL *nods to the first balloon as if to say 'See if I care if you don't want to play with me!' He blows up the second balloon. He ties a knot in the nozzle. He throws the balloon in the air. Discovers he has tied the balloon to his finger. He gets it off his finger and is now holding balloon with other hand. He throws the balloon in the air. Discovers he has tied the balloon to the finger of the other hand. He frees the balloon and at last it actually makes it into the air. He kicks the balloon. He becomes a footballer. He chalks a goalmouth on the right wall. The chalked goalmouths extend over cupboard and door. He chalks a circle in the middle of the floor. The ends of the circle don't quite meet so he boldly joins them with a straight line. He is about to kick off. Then he has a thought. He picks up the balloon and goes out through the important-looking double Door C. He returns immediately, trotting in like a world football star. He acknowledges the cheering crowds. The match begins.* WEASEL *supplies appropriate commentary in excited gobbledy-gook. He is so taken up by the game he doesn't see* PUFF *the Clown come in through Door R.* PUFF *boggles at* WEASEL. PUFF *boggles generally.* PIMPLE, *the lady clown comes in Door R.* PUFF, *seeing* PIMPLE, *converts his boggle into the look of a man who knows what's going on.*

WEASEL: . . . and he shoots!

PUFF (*catching balloon*): But Puff saves brilliantly and boots the ball to Pimple.

PUFF *kicks the balloon to* PIMPLE. *She picks up the balloon.*

PIMPLE: What a thing! Oooo! (*She cuddles balloon.*)

WEASEL: Hand ball! Penalty! Put your glasses on, Ref!

PIMPLE: I'm cuddling it. Otherwise it won't know I love it.

DRIPPENS *the clown creeps timidly in through Door R.* WEASEL *jumps on the balloon and bursts it.* DRIPPENS *shrieks in fright and flees through door R.*

You frightened him away. What a thing. Oooo.

PUFF *delivers his theory on the occurrence in twitty puff language.*

WEASEL: It was only our balloon. It popped.

No answer from DRIPPENS.

PUFF: Drippens!

WEASEL: Drippens?

PUFF: Drippens out there in your pants . . . ?

PIMPLE: Little Dripper . . .

DRIPPENS (*outside door*): Yes?

PIMPLE: You don't have to be scared. What a thing.

DRIPPENS: Who all's in there?

PIMPLE: Only Weasel and Puff.

PUFF: And Pimpole.

PIMPLE: Promise.

DRIPPENS *creeps back in. He looks around. He sees the audience. He shrieks in fright and flees back out, bawling.*

PUFF (*further theories in twitty-puff language.*)

PIMPLE: What's the matter, Little Dripper?

PUFF: In your pants?

DRIPPENS (*outside door*): You were fibbing. What's all those?

WEASEL (*pointing at audience*): He means them.

PUFF: Drippens is scared of them.

PIMPLE (*stretching out her arms and making off into the auditorium to cuddle the audience*): They're friendly and lovely and just sit there waiting for us to do things.

WEASEL *yanks her back on stage.*

DRIPPENS (*outside door*): What are they then?

PUFF: They're an audience.

WEASEL: They're naughty ants.

PUFF: Naughty ants!

PIMPLE: No, they're not naughty ants, they're nice ants.

PUFF: They're nice ants. In their pants.

DRIPPENS *comes in. He's not fully convinced.*

DRIPPENS: They're not going to do anything to me, are they? What are you?

That last question DRIPPENS *addresses to the audience. The confused reply frightens him, and once again he exits bawling.*

PUFF (*full explanation in puff-twit.*)

WEASEL: What's the matter now, Drippens?

DRIPPENS: You were fibbing. They're not ants. They don't know what they are.

PIMPLE: Well, whatever they are, they don't *do* anything.

WEASEL: Absolutely harmless and friendly. 'armless and friendly. Armless and friendly.

PUFF: Armless and friendly!

PUFF *and* WEASEL *dance the 'Armless and friendly tango-cum-gurning-ballet'.* PIMPLE *leads* DRIPPENS *into the classroom. Hand in hand. She shows him it's really quite nice in there.* DRIPPENS *and* PIMPLE *attempt the Tango.* DRIPPENS *falls into the audience.*

PIMPLE: What a thing!

As DRIPPENS *scrambles back onto the stage,* PROFESSOR MOLEREASONS *enters through the important-looking double Door C. He carries an immense book and a gamp. He hangs up the gamp and goes to desk. The clowns race to their places. They sit with legs outstretched looking up at* MOLEREASONS.

MOLEREASONS: Good morning, clowns.

CLOWNS (MOLEREASONS *conducts their response*): Good morning, Professor Molereasons.

PUFF (*in tiniest of voices, so that* MOLEREASONS *isn't sure if any-one's said anything*): In your pants!

MOLEREASONS *turns to the blackboard on the wall behind him. He writes the chapter numbers of the day on the blackboard.*

MOLEREASONS: Where exactly were we when we left off yesterday? (*He is leafing through book.* CLOWNS *look blank.*) Where exactly were we when we left off yesterday? (*The* CLOWNS *put their heads together in a huddle.*) Exactly where?

PIMPLE: Where?

MOLEREASONS: Exactly! (DRIPPENS *puts his hand up.*) Yes, Drippens, where were we then?

DRIPPENS (*pointing to an exact spot on the floor*): There!

MOLEREASONS: Wrong!

DRIPPENS (*pointing to another spot on the floor*): There?

MOLEREASONS: Wrong!

Etc., to taste.
DRIPPENS *falls into a heap under* MOLEREASON'*s desk and bawls.*

Drippens, control yourself, man! (DRIPPENS *bawls louder.*) Drippens, control yourself! (DRIPPENS *bawls even louder.*) You go too far, you do, Drippens. I am unable to work under these conditions. (MOLEREASONS *waves his stick threateningly.*) If you three don't see to it that Drippens controls himself by the time I return – swish! – whop! – wallop!

MOLEREASONS *exits through important-looking Door C., slamming it behind him.* WEASEL, PUFF *and* PIMPLE *jump up and try to cheer up* DRIPPENS. DRIPPENS *bawls louder.* PUFF *exits door L.* WEASEL *and* PIMPLE *exit Door R.* DRIPPENS *suddenly noticing there's no one there stops bawling.* PUFF *opens Door L.* DRIPPENS *sees him and bawls.* PUFF *closes door.* DRIPPENS *stops bawling.* WEASEL *opens Door R.* DRIPPENS *bawls. WEASEL closes door.* DRIPPENS *stops.* PUFF *opens his door and shuts it again very quickly.* DRIPPENS *gives short bawl while door is actually open.* PUFF *does it again.* PUFF *opens and shuts the door with* DRIPPENS *bawling accompaniment to Dum-diddle-um-dum Dum-Dum rhythm. Then* PUFF *opens the door and does a Queen Anne's Fan – sometimes called 'cocking a snoot' – at* DRIPPENS. DRIPPENS *does a Queen Anne's Fan back. Realises he's been had and says:*

DRIPPENS: I mean wah! (*Bawls.*)

CLOWNS *re-enter laughing at* DRIPPENS.

PUFF: I mean wah!!

DRIPPENS *chuckles and gurgles. The* CLOWNS *happily idiot about. Suddenly* WEASEL *has an idea.*

WEASEL: Let's have a look at the book and see exactly where we were up to when we left off yesterday.

They take the big book from the desk and thumb through it on the floor. MOLEREASONS *enters through Door C. The clowns dive for their places.* MOLEREASONS *goes to desk.*

MOLEREASONS: Where is my book? (*Despite spectacles,* MOLEREASONS *has poor eyesight.)*

PIMPLE: There!

MOLEREASONS: Where is there?

PIMPLE: There is here! (*Hopping on top of book.*)

CLOWNS *repeat the word 'here' all in a line, one behind the other till they become a train. Eventually* MOLEREASONS *sees the book.*

MOLEREASONS: Ah, here is my book! (*He picks up the book. The* CLOWNS *fall over in a heap.*) My precious book.

MOLEREASONS *returns to desk and* CLOWNS *resume their places.* MOLEREASONS *decides to launch into Chapter 31.*

Chapter thirty-one.

CLOWNS: Chapter thirty-one.

MOLEREASONS (*reading*): 'Timothy teaches the baby how to walk. A young girl passes by. She makes eyes at Timothy.' (*To* CLOWNS.) I say, are you paying attention down there, you clowns? Repeat what I just read out – that clown Weasel! (WEASEL *jumps up and gives a gross pantomime version of the Timothy saga.*) Wrong! I said repeat what I read out. (WEASEL *sits down sadly.*) That clown talking there – Puff!

PUFF *jumps up and stands in Recitation position.*

PUFF: Chapter thirty-one. Timothy teaches the baby how to walk. A young girl passes by. (MOLEREASONS *is following all this closely in the book. He gives a little grunt at each correct sentence.*) She makes pies for Timothy . . .

MOLEREASONS: No! It's 'she makes eyes at Timothy' not 'she makes pies for Timothy!' Once again – properly this time – that lady clown, Pimple!

PIMPLE *pads to desk and curtsies.*

PIMPLE: Chapter dirty-one! (*The* CLOWNS *laugh.*)

MOLEREASONS: Quiet! It's not that funny. Legs straight, Drippens!

PIMPLE: Timothy teaches the baby how to make pie. A young girl buys his pies. She likes his pies, she does. And his puddens. She likes them with gravy.

MOLEREASONS: O sit down, Pimple! As I had supposed! Now let us have everyone paying proper attention this time shall we. I shall read it out only this once twice. 'Timothy teaches the baby how to walk. A young girl passes pie' O! – er – all right, settle down – 'A young girl passes by. She makes eyes at Timothy. Timothy is flattered by this and forgets about the baby. The baby crawls off on its own, bumps into a frog and plays with it.' (MOLEREASONS *casts the drama.*) Drippens is Timothy, Weasel is the baby, Puff is the young girl and Pimple is the frog. Begin.

CLOWNS *go into cupboard and rummage out suitable props and costumes for their roles.* DRIPPENS *in his Timothy cap and coat plonks* WEASEL *in a kiddy pram.* WEASEL *does gross baby impersonation.* DRIPPENS *turfs* WEASEL *out of the pram and teaches him to walk.* PUFF *comes on with two enormous balloons as bosoms. He capers about as the young girl. He makes eyes with painted ping-pong ball halves.* MOLEREASONS *follows their actions and compares them to the book, prompting them as necessary. Timothy and the young girl get carried away. They convert the young girl's enormous bosom into an enormous bottom.* MOLEREASONS *is outraged.*

MOLEREASONS: All right, that's quite enough, thank you! Puff! Drippens! Behave yourselves! (*Meanwhile the baby and the frog are snogging.*) Weasel! Pimple! Get off each other!

MOLEREASONS *pulls them apart with a plop!* WEASEL *bites* MOLEREASONS' *top pocket hanky.*

Weasel!

MOLEREASONS *gives his verdict on the drama.*

Good in parts. Trifle vulgar in the concluding moments. Clear away.

CLOWNS *return the stuff to the cupboard.* MOLEREASONS *crosses '31' off the list on the blackboard.* CLOWNS *return to their places.*

Your undivided attention, please, Class, as we attack another chapter. Chapter twenty-seven.

CLOWNS: Chapter twenty-seven.

MOLEREASONS: Snow White. Three dwarfs creep into the castle in order to steal the mirror from Snow White's wicked stepmother. Weasel, Puff and Pimple are the three dwarfs. Drippens is the wicked Stepmother. Begin.

And it's back into the cupboard to get kitted up. WEASEL *pulls the jumper over his knees and walks on the crouch, with joke teeth and red knitted hat. He is joined by* PIMPLE *and* PUFF, *also in red hats.* PIMPLE *and* PUFF *have put shoes on their knees and are walking on their knees, carrying suitcases to hide their legs. They perform short 'lurking dwarfs' scene. From the cupboard the drama is interrupted by the sound of shattering glass.*

DRIPPENS (*in cupboard*): O no!

MOLEREASONS: Drippens, you haven't broken that mirror, have you?

DRIPPENS *emerges from cupboard with big mirror frame in which only three little fragments of actual mirror glass remain.*

DRIPPENS: Mirror, Mr Molereasons? No.

MOLEREASONS: Methinks I heard the unmistakeable noise of a Drippens breaking a mirror. If it were to turn out to be broken then I would have to be very angry. It's an exceptionally valuable item, that mirror. Explain, if you will, the sound of shattering glass?

WEASEL (*the other three having pushed him forward*): It came over ever so cold in that cupboard and my teeth started shattering.

MOLEREASONS: Are we trying to make a monkey out of Sir?

WEASEL *nods his head. He turns to others. They shake their heads. He shakes his.*

Bah! Bring that mirror here to me!

PUFF (*quietly to* DRIPPENS, *giving him similar jacket, etc., to* MOLEREASONS): Put these on, then he'll think you're what he's seeing in the mirror!

WEASEL *puts mirror frame between* MOLEREASONS *and* DRIPPENS. DRIPPENS *does everything that* MOLEREASON *does. Where* MOLEREASONS *would touch the glass he touches* DRIPPENS' *finger.* MOLEREASONS *is pretty well fooled. But something is not quite right.*

MOLEREASONS:
DRIPPENS: Curious.

PIMPLE: Shhh!

MOLEREASONS *wonders if his ears are playing tricks. He takes out his top pocket hanky to clean his ears.* DRIPPENS *panics because he hasn't got a hanky. Fortunately,* MOLEREASONS *only cleans out his ear nearest to the mirror frame, so* DRIPPENS *is able to take the other end of the hanky through the frame and thus maintain the illusion.* MOLEREASONS *breathes on the lack of glass – as of course does* DRIPPENS *– and cleans it with the hanky.* DRIPPENS *does the same on the other side.* MOLEREASONS *spits on the lack of glass. the* MOLEREASONS *gob lands on* DRIPPENS. DRIPPENS *spits back at* MOLEREASONS. *But* MOLEREASONS *outreasons the truth of the matter.*

MOLEREASONS: My spittle bounced! The mirror is all right. Funny! Heh-hee! I'd thought at first that that exceptionally costly mirror was broken. Carry on!

MOLEREASONS *gives big gesture. So does* DRIPPENS. *In doing so* DRIPPENS *knocks the mirror frame over* MOLEREASONS. MOLEREASONS *bends down to inspect the frame. Quick as a flash* WEASEL *pops a joke bald head and glasses on his head.* WEASEL *is bending down by* MOLEREASONS *so that their bald heads are together. The effect is that* WEASEL *is now* MOLEREASONS' *image.* MOLEREASONS *backs away.* WEASEL *back away.* MOLEREASONS *bumps into* PUFF, *also now in joke bald head.* MOLEREASONS *exits a deranged goof, slamming the important-looking door on the nightmare mirror world.*

PUFF (*jubilates in twitty-puff.*)

PIMPLE: What a thing! Oooo!

WEASEL: We frighted him out of his wits!

DRIPPENS: I think we taught Sir the meaning of fear.

PUFF: Professor Molereasons in your pants!

WEASEL *puts the mirror frame back in the cupboard. They are clearing away all the dwarf stuff.*

WEASEL: Sir went cuckoo, didn't he.

PIMPLE *pads off into the audience.* PIMPLE *would like to cuddle the whole audience.*

PUFF (*reports to* WEASEL *in twitty-puff that* PIMPLE *is off into the auditorium.*)

WEASEL (*running after* PIMPLE): Come back, Pimple. We'll get in terrible trouble if we get caught out here in the audimmertoreeum!

Just as WEASEL *gets her back on stage* MOLEREASONS *enters C.*

MOLEREASONS: Whatever you're doing – stop it! (CLOWNS *freeze.*) Some order here! (CLOWNS *shuffle into line.*) Some discipline! (CLOWNS *stand to attention.*) Respect! (CLOWNS *bow to* MOLEREASONS.) Sit down! (CLOWNS *sit.*) Stand up! (CLOWNS *stand.*) Sit down. (CLOWNS *sit.*) I want to speak to you clowns very seriously indeed. Instances of rudeness and lack of respect have of late been very much on the increase. In fact they have reached such an unprecedent high –

WEASEL: Hi!

MOLEREASONS: – that I am forced, Weasel, into the position of having to administer stern chastisement.

The CLOWNS *huddle together in fear.* WEASEL *eats* PUFF's *foot.* MOLEREASONS *enjoys his power.*

You will each come up here in turn and shake Sir by the hand as you solemnly promise to behave from now on in a quiet and orderly fashion

The CLOWNS *cringe themselves into a tangle. The tangle attempts to undo itself, first releasing* WEASEL. WEASEL *slowly moves towards* MOLEREASONS. MOLEREASONS *extends his hand.* WEASEL *finds that his shaking arm is paralysed. He moves it with his left slowly towards* MOLEREASONS' *hand. But it won't shake until he gets it going with the left.*

WEASEL: I promise to solemnly from now on in a quite orderly manner. I promise.

MOLEREASONS: Good boy.

WEASEL: I promise. I really really do.

PIMPLE (*who is now by* MOLEREASONS. *Taking his right hand while* WEASEL *continues to promise shaking* MOLEREASONS' *left hand*): And I promise what it is that we've got to promise too. I really promise it.

They are still shaking away as DRIPPENS *and* PUFF *arrive, to promise and shake any available bit of* MOLEREASONS' *person.* MOLEREASONS *caves in under the pressure of the promises and the clowns all pile up on top of him.*

MOLEREASONS (*from the bottom of the clown heap. Matter of factly, as if at his desk*): This is your idea of discipline, is it?

PUFF: It just seemed to happen.

MOLEREASONS: This is order, as you see it?

WEASEL: We were just a bit on the keen side perhaps.

MOLEREASONS: This is you showing respect, is it?

PIMPLE: You can never know what you're poohing till you've dung it.

MOLEREASONS (*bellowing*): You are lying on your teach-ah!

The CLOWNS *spring up and flit angelically to their places.* MOLEREASONS' *leg is twisted. He straightens it with his stick. The* CLOWNS *look so beautifully innocent that he soft-pedals.*

MOLEREASONS: You all mean well. I know that. It's just that your ever-tempestuous, effervescent temperaments are your enemies within. Well we must all fight against our enemies. Do Battle with 'em. I want you, from this moment on, to declare war on your weaknesses.

WEASEL (*brandishing imaginary sword*): War on your weaknesses!

OTHERS (*all brandishing imaginary swords*): Hurray! War!

They dive into the cupboard and instantly they're kitted up and equipped for War. They fight enthusiastically. The wounded are wrapped (tied) up in immense lengths of bandage. MOLEREASONS *retires to the comparative safety of his desk. Eventually the clowns freeze in a pose of war, as if their eager faces are saying, 'that was what you wanted wasn't it, Sir'.*

MOLEREASONS: Well, thank you very much, class, for a very excellent example of EXACTLY WHAT I DIDN'T MEAN!!! By war, I mean paying proper attention to me when I'm reading from the book! By war, I mean discipline! This is a mouth and not a noise-hole.

When MOLEREASONS *exploded the clowns bundled all the war gear back into the cupboard.* PUFF, PIMPLE *and* DRIPPENS *are sitting in legs out straight* MOLEREASONS-*approved fashion, but* WEASEL *is still in cupboard getting his bandage off.* MOLEREASONS *now notes his absence.*

Where's that clown, Weasel?

WEASEL *sitting on a bit of wood with little castors on it trundles neatly into place.*

I shall now read another chapter. Let's have every single clown giving me his/her full attention. Showing me that you've understood what we mean by war in this sense. Chapter fifty-six. Help. My aeroplane's on fire.

On the word 'help' PIMPLE *springs to her feet to help* MOLEREASONS. *She now looks for the aeroplane.*

'Chapter fifty-six. Help. My Aeroplane's on fire.' Sit down, Pimple, please. (*She sits.*) 'Three men are sitting round a pond . . .'

MOLEREASONS *leaves the desk and chalks a circle round himself on the floor. He jumps out of the 'pond' and bounds surprisingly athletically to the desk. He recaps.*

'. . . men are sitting round a pond fishing. An aeroplane streaks across the skies. It is on fire. The Pilot shrieks out "Help!"'

WEASEL (*to* PIMPLE *who is getting up again*): His aeroplane's on fire.

MOLEREASONS: Thank you. 'And he buckles on his parachute and launches himself into space. He lands right in the middle of the pond. The splash frightens all the fishes away and the Pilot is very ashamed of himself for having spoilt the anglers' fun.' Pimple, Drippens and Weasel are the three anglers. Puff is the Pilot. Begin.

The three anglers get their rods, lines and fishes out of the cupboard. Weasel's line is elastic with a ball on the end. He whangs it at the audience until MOLEREASONS *tells him to sit round the pond.* PIMPLE *forgets herself and pads into the audience.*

Audience participation is not on our curriculum, Pimple. (*Guides her back on stage.* DRIPPENS *is kissing his fish.*) Round the pond, Drippens, please. (PUFF *is on top of the cupboard with a large toy plane.*) 'Three men are sitting round a pond fishing' . . . good . . . string end of rod goes in pond, Pimple. 'An aeroplane streaks across the skies . . .'

PUFF *has got hold of a rope. He dithers for a moment and then launches himself, holding the toy plane. He swings across the stage on the rope.*

PUFF: Streakeeee-poo!

MOLEREASONS *throws a lighted match at the plane.*

MOLEREASONS: It is on fire!

PUFF: Help! My aeroplane's on fire!

PUFF *throws his aeroplane onto the floor. He lets go of the rope. He lands beside the pond. An immense parachute follows him down.*

MOLEREASONS: Parachute . . . good. Get right in the middle of the pond, Puff. He lands right in the middle of the pond.

PUFF *jumps into the pond. He spits out a jet of water which lands on* MOLEREASONS' *head.* MOLEREASONS *looks up at the roof suspecting a leak.*

I've told Mr Bogworth about that roof. (*To* PUFF.) And now the splash frightens all the fishes away.

PUFF (*picking up the fish and tossing them into the air*): Splash – splasher – splashest!

DRIPPENS *goes to the fish he was kissing. He gets a little doll's bed out of the cupboard and tucks the fish up in it. He makes to go back to the pond. But apparently the poor fish has died. He goes back to the fishbed and having listened in vain for a heartbeat he covers the head of his finny friend with the sheet.*

MOLEREASON:. . . and the Pilot is very ashamed of himself. he has spoilt the angler's fun. Go on, be very ashamed of yourself, Puff.

PUFF *sticks a finger in his mouth and exhibits profound shame. He twists his button. He pangs his dicky at himself which very nearly does him a mischief. He sinks at the knees and grovels. He blows his nose on the parachute.* MOLEREASONS *is well pleased at the display. He goes to the blackboard to give this chapter a tick. Meanwhile,* PUFF *has discovered a whole new world underneath the parachute. The other three clowns fling their rods to the wind and follow* PUFF *under the parachute.* MOLEREASONS *having ticked the chapter, is about to commence the next chapter, but then he sees four squirming shapes under the parachute.*

MOLEREASONS: All right, thank you.

The parachute becomes like an arctic tent with the four clowns' faces at the central hole.

Puff, Weasel, Pimple, Drippens! Out of there. Out you come.

The clowns experiment with the flow of the parachute.

I don't know whether you clowns have got cloth ears or what, but I told you to get out of that parachute!

The clowns become a sort of whale. The central hole of the parachute is the mouth. The whale sings 'Mammy' in the manner of Al Jolson.

Thank you very much – now just get out!

The whale turns into a chomping shark. The shark eats MOLEREASONS, *stick and all, becomes a hippo and shits out* MOLEREASONS. *The hippo turns round and belches up his stick.* MOLEREASONS *picks up his stick and threatens the clowns who are still under the parachute.*

Come along now. This silliness has gone on quite long enough. (*Aside.*) Idea. (*Aloud.*) I am unable to work under these conditions! Slam!

He slams the door but stays inside. He tiptoes to his desk and hides behind it. The clowns emerge laughing from the parachute.

MOLEREASONS (*suddenly manifesting himself at his desk*): Chapter thirty-four!

CLOWNS (*sitting down flabbergasted*): Chapter thirty-four.

MOLEREASONS (*reading*): 'The dying idiot. An old idiot lies on the point of death. He calls his three sons to his bedside and addresses them thus:'

MOLEREASONS *suddenly notices that the clowns have gone back under the parachute.*

Well, if I can't educate the top end of a clown I shall attempt to educate the bottom.

MOLEREASONS *takes a run at the clowns with his stick. Looking like a bull now under the parachute, they jump out of the way.* MOLEREASONS *takes another run at them. They dodge out of the way and* MOLEREASONS *goes hurtling out of Door L. Big crash off.* CLOWNS *emerge from under parachute. They look out of Door L.*

PUFF: He's fallen down stairs!

WEASEL: Hey!

WEASEL *gets a large cushion out of the cupboard and stuffs it under the parachute to look as if he's still under it. The others do the same.* WEASEL *speaks to the audience.*

Listen, don't give us away, will you, and if anyone in the next seat to you starts to give us away – thump 'im! (*Looking out of Door L.*) He's coming! (*The* CLOWNS *hide behind the cupboard.*)

MOLEREASONS *returns. He's got a picture round his neck. He takes it off and tosses it away. He sees what he takes to be four naughty clowns still under the parachute. He wallops in with his stick. He beats the cushions ferociously. Finally he has stopped. The forms before him suddenly look unnaturally still.*

MOLEREASONS: What have I done? Hello? Can you hear me? I'm sorry. I really am sorry – look! (*He throws his stick away.*) Was it a bit hard, was it? Why are you so quiet? It really did hurt you, did it? Please say something. O my God, I've done them in! Oh clowns! – the thing is I need you! (*Unseen by* MOLEREASONS *the clowns creep back to their places.*) There have been times when I've been wrong. There have only been times when I've been wrong. O Lord in the Sky only bring those dear clowns back to life again and I promise I will deal with their delightful if somewhat effervescent personalities (*Sees the* CLOWNS *but without fully taking in the sight.*) – Good

Morning – with love and understanding.

MOLEREASONS *boggles at the* CLOWNS *and then at the heap and then at the* CLOWNS *and then at the heap, etc., to taste and then says.*

It is you! It is you!

WEASEL: We all fall down! (*And they do. With the emotional* MOLEREASONS *on top of them.*)

MOLEREASONS: O clowns! Clowns! You just gave me a terrifying shock there. But I'm hopeful that it may have done me good, this shock. I hope I may be able to learn from it. You know what I'm going to try now? – I'm going to try these brand new teaching techniques. No Book. You are all now free to be yourselves. You can now do anything you like. Whatever you do is right. I don't stop you from doing anything. All I do is just keep very still and quiet in my corner and watch what you do and love it. Begin.

The clowns get up uncertainly. They brood. One whistles. One half-heartedly waggles his ears. A sudden snatch of song. Nothing comes to anything. And everything comes to nothing. Sulkily, they begin to clear the stage.

Er Weasel – I don't want to interfere with your self expression in any way – but what's the matter?

WEASEL: We don't know what to do.

PIMPLE: We don't know how to what.

DRIPPENS: We don't know where to how.

MOLEREASONS (*attempting humour*): I say, it's like now that you can do anything you want to you don't want to do anything!

DRIPPENS *bursts into tears. One by one the others begin to cry.*

O no! Please! Look I am unable to work under these conditions! So they don't work either, these wonderful new soft teaching techniques! I'll tell you what teaching's all about – it's about being hard! Being tough! Everything according to the book! It's about manners! Respect! Obedience! Well-bred behaviour! Fine ideals! Decorum! And above all – (*Important looking doorknob in hand.*) harsh discipline! (*Exits like thunder.*)

The CLOWNS *jump for joy. All they needed for full happiness was* MOLEREASONS' *absence.* PUFF *puts on a pair of spectacles like* MOLEREASONS' *and slams the Door C.*
The CLOWNS *dive to their places.*

PUFF (*impersonating* MOLEREASONS): I am Professor Molereasons. And I live in a holereasons. Your undivided attention please, Class, as we attack another chapter. That clown Weasel, down there in your pants, repeat what I just read out.

WEASEL *gets up. He can't remember* PUFF *having read anything out. He dithers. he sits.*

As I had supposed. Let us have everyone paying full attention, shall we. I shall read this out only twice once! 'Chapter seventy-seven.'

THE OTHERS: Chapter seventy-seven!

PUFF: The wooing.

OTHERS: The wooing.

PUFF: The woo- - -ing!

OTHERS: The woo- - -ing!

PUFF: The woo-yihihing!

OTHERS: The woo-yihihing!

PUFF (*pretending to read*): Sir Lancelump loves Lady Goonerviere. Lady Goonerviere lives at the top of a large tower. Weasel is Sir Lancelump. Pimple is Lady Goonerviere and Drippens is the Tower. Begin!

And it's cupboard time again. DRIPPENS *ferrets out a large tube of cloth up which he sticks* PROFESSOR MOLEREASONS' *umbrella. The effect is a tower.* PIMPLE *goes into the tower and climbs on* DRIPPENS' *shoulders. She cuts a window in the top of the tower with a pair of scissors.* PUFF *whispers something in her ear. She titters. He gives her a little bucket of flour.* PIMPLE *moves her lips to*

DRIPPENS' *voice.*

DRIPPENS: If only a dashing young man would come and tirra-lirra me with his lute and declare his love for me.

WEASEL *appears in knight's helmet. He's got a red carpet rolled up under his arm. He unrolls it in front of the tower.* LADY GOONERVIERE *poses suitably.*

WEASEL: What a beautiful pale skin you've got.

PIMPLE: Well, tirra-lirra me then.

WEASEL *looks lost.*

PUFF: Serenade the lady, Weasel.

WEASEL *takes out a large comb. He combs his plumes. He takes out a sandwich wrapped in tissue paper. He tosses away the sandwich and wraps the tissue round the comb and plays highlights from the 'Sheik of Araby'.* PIMPLE *pours the flour on his head and then throws the bucket at him.* WEASEL *goes to throw the bucket back at her.* PUFF *cautions him.*

PUFF: Weasel!

WEASEL: Well, if I can't kiss your beautiful pale skin I shall kiss your beautiful pail!

He kisses the bucket and then beats out a rhythm on the bucket. PUFF *pulls him off stage on the carpet, through Door L.* WEASEL *pops his head round the door to say.*

All right, this time I'm really going to impress you! (*Pops back out to ready himself.*)

PUFF (*brandishing scissors*): I am Professor Molereasons and I live in a holereasons. On my fire I put coal reasons. I don't like football because I can't see the goalreasons. My favourite music is Rock and Rollreasons. And when I die up to Heaven will go my soulreasons.

Enter WEASEL *on roller skates strumming a ukulele.* PUFF *snips* WEASEL's *braces with the scissors.* WEASEL *tap dances on the skates singing 'The Sheik of Araby'. All sing 'Ain't got no pants on' as a line by line refrain. Weasel's pants do in fact come down. The tower dances to the music.* WEASEL *suddenly sees he's actually got no pants on. By now he has skated out of them and he seeks to hide his confusion behind his ukulele. He exits Door L. Head pops round again.*

WEASEL: This time I'm really going to impress you, you fascinatin' witch!

PUFF *has an idea and hands a witch mask and rose to* PIMPLE.

Enter weasel on roller skates

PUFF: Hurry up Weasel out there in your pants. Or rather, not in your pants. I am unable to work under these conditions. I am unable to lurk under these conditions. I am unable to Turk under these conditions and I am unable to jerk under these conditions and I am unable to perk under these conditions and I am unable to quirk under these conditions and I am unable to murk under these conditions.

WEASEL *roars in on a motorbike. He does a flashy circuit or two. He pulls up beneath the tower. He has a toy sax mounted on the handlebars. He serenades Lady Goonerviere on sax, hooter and revs – a Strauss Waltz.* PIMPLE *throws him the rose as one in love.*

WEASEL: A rose! Lady Goonerviere loves me! (*The rose squirts him in the face.*)

PIMPLE *moves her lips to* DRIPPENS' *voice.*

DRIPPENS: Yes, I love you and I come to you.

She collapses the umbrella and the tower of cloth to reveal a giant woman in a hideous witch mask. Terrified, WEASEL *kicks the motorbike into gear and is about to roar out through the double doors just as* MOLEREASONS *comes back in. He turns the motorbike back the other way –* MOLEREASONS *has leapt back out into the corridor – but once again* WEASEL *encounters the hideous giant witch woman. He panics.* MOLEREASONS *chases him.* MOLEREASONS *manages to catch hold of a strap on the back of the motorbike.* MOLE-

REASONS *falls on his back and* WEASEL *drives them through the classroom wall. Bricks and plaster and dust and filth fly into the air.* MOLEREASONS *re-enters through the hole in the wall. He is coughing and sneezing.*

MOLEREASONS: I just go out for two minutes and look what happens! Let's have some order here! Some quiet! Some discipline! (DRIPPENS *is building up to a big sneeze.*) Don't sneeze! (DRIPPENS *is about to bawl.*) And don't bawl.

WEASEL *returns through the hole in the wall. There is a brick stuck in his helmet. And a bit of an exhaust pipe in his socks.*

A public apology for this outrage – Puff!

PUFF (*still impersonating* MOLEREASONS): A public apology for this outrage – Puff!

MOLEREASONS: Bah!

MOLEREASONS *tries to strike* PUFF *but he brains the already dizzy* WEASEL.

A public apology begins with the word 'Sir'. Once again, properly this time – Weasel doesn't seem quite up to it – the lady clown, Pimple.

PIMPLE *goes up to* MOLEREASONS' *desk, curtsies and says.*

PIMPLE: Dear Professor Molereasons Sir. We wish to make it clear that we are extremely sorry for the outrage, and it was an outrage, and that's why you're inraged because we out-raged, and we won't do it ever again, if only you Sir, in your big mercy could just forgive us, just this once . . . oh, go on, Sir . . . and we will be good for ever and always. Amen.

During the public apology PIMPLE *has been nervously fiddling with the button of her jacket. In fact she has nervously fiddled it into the button-hole of* MOLEREASONS' *jacket.*

MOLEREASONS: Good. Thank you. Chapter thirty-four.

CLOWNS: Chapter thirty four.

MOLEREASONS (*reading*): 'The dying idiot. An old idiot lies on the point of death. He calls his three sons to his bedside and addresses them thus . . .' (MOLEREASONS *is suddenly aware of* PIMPLE *fiddling with his jacket button.*) Pimple, go and sit down! What on earth are you at, woman? Are you asking to have your head squeezed? This is a continuing naughtiness while Sir is actually trying to read from the book.

PIMPLE *has now taken off her jacket which is now dangling from* MOLEREASONS' *jacket buttonhole. She sits down in her shirt.*

A naughtiness of that order deserves severe chastisement!

MOLEREASONS *strides towards* PIMPLE *but trips over her jacket. His book flies out of his hands and he knocks himself out on the floor.*

PIMPLE: What a thing! Eh? Ooo.

DRIPPENS: Bad luck there, Sir!

WEASEL: Poor old Sir!

The CLOWNS *try to get* MOLEREASONS *up. First they put him on his head. Then they drop him back again. Now they put him on his feet. He falls forward and they catch him. He falls backwards. They catch him. He falls forward into* PUFF's *arms.* PUFF *carries him to the desk. But he puts him at the desk the wrong way. As soon as* PUFF *leaves him he falls forward with his head resting on the blackboard.* PUFF *turns him round the right way. He models* MOLEREASONS *into one of his typical teaching postures. He gives him a pointing finger. He puts* MOLEREASONS' *finger up his nose then takes it out and makes it point at the clowns. He twists* MOLEREASONS' *mouth into his customary scowl. He sits down. They all wait to see if anything happens. It doesn't.* WEASEL *picks up the book and takes it to the desk. He converts* MOLEREASONS' *pointing-at-the-clowns finger into a pointing-at-a-passage-in-the-book finger. He tilts* MOLEREASONS' *head forward so he seems to be reading. He sits down. Nothing happens.* DRIPPENS *puts* MOLEREASONS' *stick in his*

other hand and models him into a threatening pose with it. Sits. Nothing. PIMPLE *gets up and clouts* MOLEREASONS *on the back. Life returns to the Professor.*

MOLEREASONS: Good morning, clowns.

CLOWNS: Good morning, Professor Molereasons!

MOLEREASONS: Chapter thirty-one.

CLOWNS: Chapter thirty-FOUR.

Bell sounds.

PUFF: Breaktime, Sir!

MOLEREASONS: Breaktime! But we've only been here a minute!

But the clowns charge out to the playground.

What's happening? I must get a grip of myself.

MOLEREASONS *scratches his head. He exits through important looking Door C.*

Interval

Act Two

The CLOWNS *return to the classroom. Followed, seconds later, by* PROFESSOR MOLEREASONS.

MOLEREASONS: 'Chapter thirty-four'.

CLOWNS: Chapter thirty-four.

MOLEREASONS (*reading*): 'The dying idiot. An old idiot lies on the point of death. He calls his three sons to his bedside and addresses them thus: 'Whichever one of you can make me laugh the most to him will I leave everything.' Puff is the dying idiot. You others are the three sons. Begin. (PUFF *gets mattress out of the cupboard.*) A chance for you to really let yourselves go in this one, class. In this one you're meant to be funny!

MOLEREASONS *assists* PUFF *into character and situation.*

'An old (PUFF *does his old.*)
idiot (PUFF *adds idiot.*)
lies (PUFF *lies.*)
on the point (PUFF *goes 'ouch' as if pricked in bum.*)
of death' (PUFF *attempts to look poorly.*)

PUFF (*in character of old idiot*): My sons, my sons, my time is almost comeblebum. Come into my bedroom, boys, that I may speak with 'ee.

The sons mime coming in through door one by one. WEASEL *is last. He can't open the imaginary door, so he goes through the wall to the other side, opens it, goes back through hole and then comes in through door.*

I want 'ee to make me laugh my last laugh and that right hoarsely. (WEASEL *whinnies.*) So let's cut the cackle and jest get on with it. Jest get on with it! The son who makes me laugh the most shall have all my puds and chapels. Right, son the first, standing there in your pants, make me laugh. (DRIPPENS *as son the first makes silly faces.*) I don't get it. (PIMPLE *as son the second makes silly faces at father.*) I don't get it. (WEASEL *does funny faces and silly walks.*) I don't get it. (*The old idiot suddenly notices* PROFESSOR MOLEREASONS.) O yes! Now that's what I calls funny!

He laughs hysterically at MOLEREASONS' *face. In his hysteria he summons* WEASEL *to his side.*

WEASEL: Shhhh! Daddy wants to tell us something.

PIMPLE: What's he saying?

WEASEL (*reporting what* PUFF *is whispering and snickering into his ear*): He says that him over there – the charming gentleman in the horn-rimmed spectacles – has won the funniest face competition and therefore inherits everything Dad's got.

PIMPLE: What all's he gonna get then?

WEASEL (*as* PUFF *whispers further*): A castle – he's going to get a castle – a knight's castle.

DRIPPENS: Oo, a knight's castle.

PUFF: Knight's Castle Soap – but it fell on the floor and got all hairs in it!

The old idiot laughs himself to death. He dies with his arms and legs sticking up in the air. WEASEL *gives one leg a little push and the stiff, dead idiot falls on his side.*

MOLEREASONS: Well, that was beginning to border on impertinence . . . It's a good job I'm a sport.

MOLEREASONS *laughs. He laughs right into the clowns' faces. At first they think all is well. But then* MOLEREASONS' *continuing maniacal laughter begins to frighten them. They seek refuge under the mattress pursued by the laughing, clearly demented,* MOLEREASONS.

You're all so funny, aren't you, you clowns! Drippens! (*Laughs and grossly impersonates* DRIPPENS.) Pimple! (*Laughs and grossly impersonates* PIMPLE.) Weasel! (*Laughs and grossly impersonates* WEASEL.) Puff!

He really goes to town on PUFF. *But gradually* MOLEREASONS' *laughter turns to tears. He exits Door C., weeping profusely.*
Four worried clowns creep out from under the mattress.

PIMPLE: What a thing. Was he serious?

PUFF: It was a fit. Fits last three minutes and then that's it and they don't come back.

WEASEL: I hope you're right.

PIMPLE: I think we were a bit horrible to him. We definitely weren't lovely.

PUFF: Yes, but he's not lovely.

PIMPLE: If we were lovely to him he would be lovely to us.

DRIPPENS: What do you have to do to be lovely?

PIMPLE: This sort of thing. (*She pads up to* DRIPPENS *and kisses him.*)

WEASEL: Pimple loves Drippens!

PUFF (*to* DRIPPENS): A Gent would return that kiss.

DRIPPENS: Really?

WEASEL: Do you want to break the heart of your beloved?

DRIPPENS: No.

PUFF: Well, get in there and kiss her.

DRIPPENS (*shyly going over to* PIMPLE): No, not while you're looking.

PUFF: Obviously we shall look the other way while you actually do it.

DRIPPENS: Promise?

WEASEL: Yes, we'll look the other way. Promise.

PUFF *and* WEASEL *demonstrate looking the other way.*

DRIPPENS: You're peeping!

WEASEL: No we wasn't, was we?

PUFF: Nor we! (*Actually they were.*) We'll hide behind the cupboard. (*They get behind cupboard.*) Now go on and kiss her. You mustn't keep a Lady waiting.

DRIPPENS *kisses* PIMPLE. PIMPLE *pads joyfully into the auditorium to share her happiness with the audience.*

PUFF & WEASEL: Drippens loves Pimple!

DRIPPENS: You did peep!

DRIPPENS *wants a little hand mirror from the cupboard. he slings open the cupboard door which bashes into the faces of* PUFF *and* WEASEL, *trapping them, dazed, behind the open cupboard door. He looks at his cheek in the little mirror. He paints large lipstick lips on his white cheek. He puts mirror back in cupboard. He shuts cupboard door. The stiff bodies of* PUFF *and* WEASEL *fall head first to the ground.* DRIPPENS *stands about being in love.* WEASEL *comes to. He sees that* PIMPLE *is in the auditorium. He goes after her egged on by twitty-puff warnings from* PUFF.

WEASEL: Come back, Pimple. You know you mustn't be out here. (*Grabbing her and dragging her back.*) It's Sir you said you wanted to be lovely to.

PIMPLE: I was practising being lovely.

WEASEL: Well, practise on Sir.

PIMPLE (*now back on stage*): The Practice of Love.

DRIPPENS *is hidden away with his own thoughts in a corner.* MOLEREASONS *enters C.* WEASEL *and* PUFF *dive to their places.* PIMPLE *vamps towards* MOLEREASONS. *She kisses* MOLEREASONS.

MOLEREASONS: Pimple! What on earth's the game, Woman!

PIMPLE: We weren't being lovely to you and now we want to be lovely to you.

MOLEREASONS: No! No! You mustn't! There mustn't be any of that, thank you!

PIMPLE: What a THING. (*She sits down.*)

MOLEREASONS (*regaining composure. Goes to desk. Opens book*): 'Chapter –' where is Drippens?

PUFF:
WEASEL: Chapter where is Drippens.
PIMPLE:

MOLEREASONS: No. No. Where is Drippens?

WEASEL: He's gone off.

MOLEREASONS: Gone off?

PUFF (*miming dynamite explosion*): Gone off!

WEASEL: Gone off! (*Miming pong.*)

MOLEREASONS: Bah!

PUFF: Actually, Sir, he's in love.

MOLEREASONS: In love!

DRIPPENS *dances from his hiding place. A ballet of one in love. He dances to his place.* MOLEREASONS *points at lipstick mark on* DRIPPENS' *cheek.*

Drippens, who gave you that? Speak out loud and fearlessly, lad.

DRIPPENS: I have found true love, Sir.

MOLEREASONS: Love is undoubtedly a many splendoured thing, Drippens – but beware you don't fool with it lest it fool with you. (*This last warning triggers off an old sorrow in* MOLEREASONS' *memory. He forgets entirely where he is as he murmurs.*) Mabel!

He kisses the lost Mabel of his mind. He realises that he is in a classroom of clowns and not the boudoir of Mabel.

Right, class, I think it will be the best thing for all of us if we put all our concentration into the reading of the next chapter. (*He mops his brow.*) 'Chapter one hundred and three.'

CLOWNS: Chapter One hundred and three.

MOLEREASONS (*reading*): 'The Incredibly Wealthy Baron Grabbit requires a new servant. Three men are on the short list for the position. Baron Grabbit will choose the most humble, grovelling and toadying of the three.' Weasel is the first applicant. Pimple is the second applicant, and Drippens.

PIMPLE: Is the third applicant.

MOLEREASONS: Thank you and Puff is the Baron. Begin.

PUFF: I am the Incredibly Wealthy Baron Grabbit in my pants. Come over here, worm! Go over there worm! Speak up! Be quiet! I can't hear you! Shut up! Bum! Bum-bum! Bogies!

MOLEREASONS: All right, thank you, Puff. I don't think you've quite got hold of the character of the Baron there. The Baron is an old time gentleman – he walks like an old time gentleman –

MOLEREASONS *hitches up his trousers and demonstrates calf-conscious Restoration style walking.* PUFF *attempts to do it.*

– and he talks like an old time gentleman – (MOLEREASONS *gives* PUFF *his stick to aid his characterisation.)*

PUFF: Please. Thank you. A drop more tea, mother?

MOLEREASONS: Yes, that's more the idea. (MOLEREASONS *now addresses the three applicants.*) Now the humble and grovelling applicants, apart from general toadying will of course have to master the art of flattery. Thus it will emerge that one of you is better than the others. Begin. First applicant, Weasel. Go on, out you go.

MOLEREASONS *pushes* WEASEL *out of the Door C.* WEASEL *knocks on door.* BARON *gives gentlemanly wave of stick, indicating 'come in'.* WEASEL *squashes his face against the glass of the important looking Door C.* WEASEL *knocks again.*

PUFF (*roaring*): Well come in!

WEASEL (*comes in. Speaking very quickly and physically mawling the Baron in his enthusiasm to be toadiest*): God bless you, good morning and good afternoon, Baron Grabbit sir, so wonderful of you to say COME IN in such a delightfully baronial tone of voice, that noise of COME IN was music to my ears, and your feet if I may say so are perfume to my nose.

PUFF (*as* BARON): Who are you and what do you want?

WEASEL: Who am I? I'm nothing, a nobody, a no one. I'm a sausage.

A teeny weeny sausage. In fact I'm not even a sausage. I'm the skin of a sausage. I'm the skin of a skinless sausage. I'm just a bit of left-overs on somebody's plate.

PUFF: What do you want?

WEASEL: What do I want? I want a job as your grovelling servant, and I've come all this way, O go on, give us a job, Puffy . . .

PUFF: Not bad.

WEASEL: Not bad! (*He jumps for joy into Puff's arms and kisses him.*)

PUFF: Get off! Get off! Just sit down over there until I've made my decision. Next.

MOLEREASONS: Next applicant – Pimple! (*But* PIMPLE *is sitting hand in hand with* DRIPPENS, *dreaming into his eyes.*) Pimple! (*She goes to the door.*) This is a classroom not a cinema!

PIMPLE *knocks on the inside of the door.*

PUFF: Come in!

PIMPLE *goes out. She knocks from outside.*

Come in!

She comes in backwards. She turns round and traps her fingers in the door.

PIMPLE: Yaaahhhhhhh (*Pain now turning into worship of the Baron.*) Ooooooooooo Mr Baboon Sir, I am dazzled by your beaming face, I want to be your humble and grovelly grovelly servant, you can do what you like with me, you can kick me. (*She picks up his leg and makes it kick her.*) O Mr Baboon, please give me the job –

PUFF: O please don't cry on my socks, Woman.

PIMPLE *rises and bows deeply.* PUFF *measures the depth of the bow with the stick.* DRIPPENS *takes note.*

Not bad. (*Referring to the measurement of bow depth as recorded on the stick.*)

PIMPLE: O Mr Baboon.

PUFF: Yes, well you just sit down there dear, till I've seen the rest of the applicants. Next.

MOLEREASONS: Drippens!

DRIPPENS (*goes straight up to Baron.* DRIPPENS' *theory is that it's all down to bow-depth*): My name is Harold Humblebum and I would like to be your toadying and grovelling servant. Shall I grovel now?

PUFF: In your own time.

DRIPPENS: And you'll measure how low on the grovelling stick. How low.

PUFF: How low.

WEASEL: Hello! (*Waving.*)

MOLEREASONS: Shut up, Weasel!

DRIPPENS: All right – here I go now. Grovelling and toadying. Are you ready with your stick?

PUFF: Yes.

DRIPPENS *bows.* PUFF *measures depth.*

DRIPPENS: How was I?

PUFF: Not as good as the last man.

DRIPPENS *has another go.*

No.

DRIPPENS *really grovels like a goodun. A hole opens up in the floor and he falls through.*

PUFF: That's my man! Definitely!

WEASEL: A toad in the hole!

MOLEREASONS *peers down hole and then goes to Door C., to see if Mr Bogworth is anywhere about.*

PUFF: Well don't just sit there! Fish my servant out of the hole!

The two applicants yank DRIPPENS *out of the hole. He is unconscious. They listen to his heart.*

WEASEL: He's dead. He bowed so low he broke his neck!

PUFF: Dead! My servant dead!

WEASEL (*grabbing Puff's stick*): Let's be your servant then, Puffy.

PIMPLE: No, me!

WEASEL: What sort of humble and grovelling servant do you think you're going to make, bum-face?

PIMPLE: More grumble and hovelling than you, pongy-drawers!

PIMPLE *and* WEASEL *are fighting for Puff's stick. But* PUFF *is still holding on tight.*

MOLEREASONS: Pimple! Weasel!

The fight for possession of the stick pangs PUFF *towards the hole.* PUFF *falls down hole.*

Puff! O no.

WEASEL: Now look what you did.

PIMPLE: You did it, you mean.

WEASEL *is panged down hole.*

MOLEREASONS: Weasel!

PIMPLE *jumps down hole.* MOLEREASONS *picks up stick.*

O Lord in the sky help me to find the words to express myself at this outrage!

DRIPPENS *is lying inert with his feet towards the hole.* MOLEREASONS *stands between* DRIPPENS' *feet and the hole, peering down into the depths.*

Come out of that hole, you clowns.

Life returns to DRIPPENS. *He stretches his legs pushing* PROFESSOR MOLEREASONS *down the hole. We hear the* PROFESSOR*'s voice coming up from under the earth.*

Drippens, this is Professor Molereasons attempting to contact Drippens the clown from this hole!

DRIPPENS: Ooh there's a hole here!

MOLEREASONS: Drippens, pull me out.

DRIPPENS: Pull your what?

MOLEREASONS: Out! Get hold of the stick! (MOLEREASONS' *stick appears up through the hole.*)

DRIPPENS: Get hold of the what?

MOLEREASONS: The stick! (DRIPPENS *gets hold of it.*) And whatever you do, Drippens, don't let go! (MOLEREASONS' *red face appears up hole.*)

DRIPPENS: Don't what?

MOLEREASONS: Let go! (DRIPPENS *lets go.*) Yahhhhhhhh! (MOLEREASONS *disappears back down hole.*)

DRIPPENS: Oo I dropped Professor Molereasons down the hole. Oo-er. Poor old Drippens. What am I going to do now? I'll get into trouble for that, won't I (*To audience.*) Where could I hide? (*Wherever is suggested on stage* DRIPPENS *thinks of snags. Eventually he or the audience decide he should hide in the auditorium.*) You won't give me away, will you?

The other three clowns and MOLEREASONS *come up through the hole.* MOLEREASONS *has to be assisted with* WEASEL *pushing his rump and* PUFF *hauling on the stick.*

MOLEREASONS: Go on! Ah! Good. Now you clowns just keep well away from that hole until poor Mr Bogworth can get it mended. Where is Drippens?

PUFF: Somewhere else.

WEASEL: Gone to town.

PIMPLE: A gone down town clown.

PUFF: And you've got a frown because he's a gone down town clown.

PIMPLE: And you've got a brown frown because he's a gone down town clown in a white gown.

WEASEL: And you've got a brown frown because he's a gone down town clown in a white gown with his knickers hanging down!

MOLEREASONS: All right, that's quite enough thank you. Drippens, where are you? Drippens, if you don't come back here immediately your punishment will be too frightful to contemplate! Bah! Find Drippens!

PUFF, PIMPLE *and* WEASEL *chase in and out of the three doors, the cupboard and the hole in the wall, looking for* DRIPPENS. MOLEREASONS *falls down the hole in the floor. As he tries to get out, the three clowns run over his head without seeing him. The three clowns are off-stage as* MOLEREASONS *scrabbles and heaves himself out of the hole.*

MOLEREASONS: Drippens, when I find you I'm going to wallop you into next year!

DRIPPENS (*from auditorium*): O no.

MOLEREASONS: Drippens, you're out there in the auditorium.

DRIPPENS: Yes!

MOLEREASONS (*getting large torch out of the cupboard*): Have I lifted the ban on going into the auditorium?

DRIPPENS: Yes.

MOLEREASONS (*scanning the audience with torch*): Have I not rather taken great pains to stress the undesirability of going into the audience . . . ?

DRIPPENS: Yes – no – yes.

MOLEREASONS (*spotting* DRIPPENS): Come back up here immediately, you wretched clown.

DRIPPENS (*two steps stagewards one step back*): No yes yes no etc.

MOLEREASONS: Drippens, hurry up! (*Unseen by* MOLEREASONS *the other three clowns go into the audience.*) Drippens, lad, do you hear that racket the audience is making? They are indignant at your gross behaviour! Your unpardonable behaviour is already beginning to affect large pockets of the audience! Drippens get a grip of yourself! Up you come, you miserable, naughty, nasty little clown! (DRIPPENS *is now on-stage.*) What have you to say in your defence? (DRIPPENS *howls.*) Don't howl – speak! Are you afraid?

DRIPPENS: Yes!

MOLEREASONS: I want the truth now, Drippens – you are definitely frightened by me and my old fashioned teaching methods . . . ?

DRIPPENS: Yes.

MOLEREASONS: Well, that's good, Drippens. That is how it ought to be. Authorities agree that fear and concentration go hand in hand. I shall use you as an example, Drippens, an example to the other three, but they're not here either!!! O this is too silly! I am unable to work under these conditions! (MOLEREASONS *exits C., slamming door.*)

DRIPPENS (*happily*): Whoo – hoo Pimple!

PIMPLE (*from audience*): Whoo – hoo Little Dripper!

MOLEREASONS (*barging back in*): Drippens, I'm holding you personally responsible to see to it that those other three clowns are back in here by the time I return. If they're not back here by the time I return your punishment will be frightful – I shall tear off your pom-poms! (*Exits C. slamming door.*)

DRIPPENS: You've got to come back here.

WEASEL: No, I'm going to stay with the kids.

PIMPLE: We're being lovely with them.

DRIPPENS: But he's gonna tear off me pom-poms.

PUFF: Stick your pom-poms on his desk and get down here.

DRIPPENS: O please stop it. Please come back or I'm going to get into terrible trouble.

PIMPLE: Come down here, Little Dripper!

DRIPPENS: It's all right for you down there having a good time, I mean I'm glad you're down there having a good time it's just that if I was down there having a good time I wouldn't be having a good time at all because I'd be thinking all the time of what terrible trouble little Drippens is going to get into when he gets back here.

MOLEREASONS (*barging back in*): One more thing, Drippens, the next chapter will be a test chapter and we know what that means, don't we?

MOLEREASONS *chuckles maniacally, forgets to open the door and bashes into it. He goes sprawling. His spectacles come off. He wanders blindly about the stage, tapping his way with his stick.*

Can you see my spectacles anywhere, please, Drippens?

DRIPPENS (*finds the spectacles. Wonders whether to give them back or not. Eventually he decides he will*): Here you are, Sir.

MOLEREASONS: Thank you.

He puts them on. But he's still almost blind. He discovers that the glass has come out of them. Enraged.

This unfortunate mishap has put me in an even worse mood for your test chapter! (*He fumbles his way to the door and exits.*)

PIMPLE: What a thing – eh?

PUFF (*twitty-puffs.*)

WEASEL (*climbing back on stage followed by the other two*): So it's shitty old test time!

PIMPLE: We've dung it now.

DRIPPENS: I'm frightened!

PIMPLE: It's all right, Little Dripper – we'll get through it somehow.

They form a tableau of irrational hope against unconquerable odds.

PUFF: But how?

DRIPPENS: Only a miragical could save us now.

PIMPLE (*an amazing idea has occurred to her*): What a thing! Yes. Yes. What a thing!

WEASEL: What? What?

PUFF: What?

PIMPLE (*referring to audience*): If they all come up here – they could help us with the test –

PUFF: We could paint them up as clowns!

WEASEL: Brilliant!

PUFF: Come on, up you come, clowns!!!

As the audience arrives on stage the clowns form a clown painting factory. PUFF *keeps checking the double door C., to make sure* MOLEREASONS *is no longer about.* MR BOGWORTH *has now mended the hole in the floor.*

PUFF: Right, sit down, clowns – here he comes!

MOLEREASONS (*enters, still almost blind. Taps his way to his desk*): Right, I want to speak to you four clowns very seriously. Do you know what you made me do? You got me in such a rage that you made me break my glasses, and I had to take them all the way up the road to the opticians, groping my way, lamp-post by lamp-post, making a complete spectacle of myself – quiet! – and the optician says he won't be able to mend them for a while, so I can't see you very well – but I think I can see you four wretched clowns well enough to give you your test chapter!

His nose is literally on the book, so close he has to be to the print to read it.

And your test chapter is one of the very difficult chapters, 'Chapter fifteen.'

CLOWNS & CHILDREN: Chapter fifteen!

MOLEREASONS: Curious! A multi-ventriloquial trick, eh? Made your voices sound like a crowd . . . Hmmm . . . well there we are, examination nerves provide us with miracles. Full concentration class on your test chapter – 'Chapter fifteen' –

CLOWNS & CHILDREN: Chapter fifteen!

MOLEREASONS: The first time was funny! (*Reading.*) 'The Wild Riders. The good people of the Westmorlands are in the grip of a sleeping sickness. It has sent them all stupid of head and dull of brain. Honest Arthur, Jumping Joe Soap and Moaning Mungo Wiggins go galloping through the Westmorlands trying to wake up the inhabitants.' Puff is honest Arthur, Weasel is Jumping Joe Soap. Pimple is Moaning Mungo Wiggins –

PIMPLE: And Drippens is the Westmorlands!

MOLEREASONS: Idiot interruptions are not going to help you pass your examination. Let us just consider this chapter for a moment. I think the point at issue here is the immensity of area of the Westmorlands, which is to say that if you don't make enough noise the good people of the Westmorlands are going to remain stupid of head and dull of brain and you'll all fail your examination and we know what that means don't we! All right – off you go, Wild Riders! Begin!

EVERYONE: Wake up! Etc.

An incredible racket. MOLEREASONS *is amazed and incredibly pleased.*

MOLEREASONS: Thank you. That was good. It was more than good – it was excellent! You've never been as good as that in a test chapter before. I shall have to give you all ten out of ten. Four ten out of tens. I shall re-instate the box of sticky gold stars. I see this as a great triumph for old fashioned teaching techniques – and an example to slack modern methods.

MR BOGWORTH *fights his way to the Professor.*

BOGWORTH: Professor! Professor!

MOLEREASONS: Who's that? Mr Bogworth, is it? Yes, Mr Bogworth, what can we do for you?

BOGWORTH: The optician's finished your glasses, Professor.

MOLEREASONS: Well that is excellent!

BOGWORTH *puts the glasses into the hand of the almost blind* MOLEREASONS.

The glasses finshed and Class is finished!

MOLEREASONS *puts specs on and sees painted audience in his classroom. he takes them off.*

I say, Mr Bogowrth, I think the glass is dirty . . .

BOGWORTH: No, it's not dirty, Professor.

MOLEREASONS (*putting them on again*): Has the wretched man put trick multiplying glass in?

BOGWORTH: No, he's put perfectly ordinary glasses glass in your glasses, Professor.

MOLEREASONS (*goes and inspects painted audience. Finally his conclusion*): I'd like you four clowns to pay attention to what I've got to say to you. Wherever I look all I can see is nasty little Westmorlanders. I think the only deduction we can make is that I am batty . . . certainly off my conk to a degree . . . I think I shall definitely call class over for today . . . (*As he shuffles off.*) . . . I think what I shall do is go home, put my slippers on, and have a cup of tea . . .

The curtain falls.

Methuen Young Drama

RARE EARTH
a programme about pollution
devised by Belgrade Coventry
Theatre in Education Company
for 9-11 year-olds

SWEETIE PIE
a play about women in society
devised by Bolton Octagon Theatre in
Education Company, edited and introduced
by Eileen Murphy
for 14 year-olds upwards

OLD KING COLE
a play by Ken Campbell
originally written for the Victoria Theatre,
Stoke-on-Trent
for 8-12 year-olds

SKUNGPOOMERY
a play by Ken Campbell
for 7-13 year-olds

TIMESNEEZE
a participatory play by
David Campton
originally written by the Young Vic
for 7-11 year-olds

THE ADVENTURES OF AWFUL KNAWFUL
a play by Peter Flannery and
Mick Ford originally written as
the RSC Kids' Show
for 7-11 year-olds

THE INCREDIBLE VANISHING!!!
a play by Denise Coffey
originally written for the
Young Vic
for 8-12 year-olds

PONGO PLAYS 1-6
six short plays by
Henry Livings with music by
Alex Glasgow
for 12 year-olds upwards

SIX MORE PONGO PLAYS
six short plays by Henry Livings
with music by Alex Glasgow
for 12 year-olds upwards

THEATRE-IN-EDUCATION PROGRAMMES: INFANTS
edited by Pam Schweitzer
five programmes for 5-8 year-olds

THEATRE-IN-EDUCATION PROGRAMMES: JUNIORS
edited by Pam Schweitzer
four programmes for 8-12 year-olds

THEATRE-IN-EDUCATION PROGRAMMES: SECONDARY
edited by Pam Schweitzer
four programmes for 12 year-olds
upwards

PLAYSPACE
four plays edited by
Michael Kustow
for 8-14 year-olds
(**The Cutting of Marchan Wood**
by Richard M. Hughes;
The Boy Without a Head
by Edward Lucie-Smith;
Tamburlane the Mad Hen
by Adrian Mitchell;
The Legend of Scarface and Blue Water
by Niki Marvin)

Methuen's Modern Plays

Jean Anouilh	*Antigone*
	Becket
	The Lark
John Arden	*Serjeant Musgrave's Dance*
	The Workhouse Donkey
	Armstrong's Last Goodnight
John Arden and	*The Business of Good Government*
Margaretta D'Arcy	*The Royal Pardon*
	The Hero Rises Up
	The Island of the Mighty
	Vandaleur's Folly
Wolfgang Bauer	*Shakespeare the Sadist*
Rainer Werner Fassbinder	*Bremen Coffee,*
Peter Handke	*My Foot My Tutor,*
Frank Xaver Kroetz	*Stallerhof*
Brendan Behan	*The Quare Fellow*
	The Hostage
	Richard's Cork Leg
Edward Bond	*A-A-America!* and *Stone*
	Saved
	Narrow Road to the Deep North
	The Pope's Wedding
	Lear
	The Sea
	Bingo
	The Fool and *We Come to the River*
	Theatre Poems and Songs
	The Bundle
	The Woman
	The Worlds with *The Activists Papers*
	Restoration and *The Cat*
	Summer
Bertolt Brecht	*Mother Courage and Her Children*
	The Caucasian Chalk Circle
	The Good Person of Szechwan
	The Life of Galileo
	The Threepenny Opera
	Saint Joan of the Stockyards
	The Resistible Rise of Arturo Ui
	The Mother

	Mr Puntila and His Man Matti
	The Measures Taken and other Lehrstücke
	The Days of the Commune
	The Messingkauf Dialogues
	Man Equals Man and *The Elephant Calf*
	The Rise and Fall of the City of Mahagonny and *The Seven Deadly sins*
	Baal
	A Respectable Wedding and other one-act plays
	Drums in the Night
	In the Jungle of Cities
Howard Brenton	*The Churchill Play*
	Weapons of Happiness
	Epsom Downs
	The Romans in Britain
	Plays for the Poor Theatre
	Magnificence
	Revenge
	Hitler Dances
Howard Brenton and David Hare	*Brassneck*
Shelagh Delaney	*A Taste of Honey*
	The Lion in Love
David Edgar	*Destiny*
	Mary Barnes
Michael Frayn	*Clouds*
	Alphabetical Order and *Donkey's Years*
	Make and Break
Max Frisch	*The Fire Raisers*
	Andorra
	Triptych
Simon Gray	*Butley*
	Otherwise Engaged and other plays
	Dog Days
	The Rear Column and other plays
	Close of Play and *Pig in a Poke*
	Stage Struck
	Quartermaine's Terms
Peter Handke	*Offending the Audience* and *Self-Accusation*
	Kaspar

The Ride Across Lake Constance
They Are Dying Out

Barrie Keeffe
Gimme Shelter (Gem, Gotcha, Getaway)
Barbarians (Killing Time, Abide With Me, In the City)
A Mad World, My Masters

Arthur Kopit
Indians
Wings

John McGrath
The Cheviot, the Stag and the Black, Black Oil

David Mercer
After Haggerty
The Bankrupt and other plays
Cousin Vladimir and *Shooting the Chandelier*
Duck Song
The Monster of Karlovy Vary and *Then and Now*
No Limits To Love

Peter Nichols
Passion Play
Poppy

Joe Orton
Loot
What the Butler Saw
Funeral Games and *The Good and Faithful Servant*
Entertaining Mr Sloane
Up Against It

Harold Pinter
The Birthday Party
The Room and *The Dumb Waiter*
The Caretaker
A Slight Ache and other plays
The Collection and *The Lover*
The Homecoming
Tea Party and other plays
Landscape and *Silence*
Old Times
No Man's Land
Betrayal
The Hothouse

Luigi Pirandello
Henry IV
Six Characters in Search of an Author

Stephen Poliakoff
Hitting Town and *City Sugar*

David Rudkin
The Sons of Light
The Triumph of Death

Jean-Paul Sartre	*Crime Passionnel*
Wole Soyinka	*Madmen and Specialists*
	The Jero Plays
	Death and the King's Horseman
C.P. Taylor	*And a Nightingale Sang . . .*
	Good
Nigel Williams	*Line 'Em*
	Class Enemy
Charles Wood	*Veterans*
Theatre Workshop	*Oh What a Lovely War!*
Various authors	*Best Radio Plays of 1978* (Don Haworth: *Episode on a Thursday Evening:* Tom Mallin: *Halt! Who Goes There?;* Jennifer Phillips: *Daughters of Men;* Fay Weldon: *Polaris;* Jill Hyem: *Remember Me;* Richard Harris: *Is It Something I Said?)*
	Best Radio Plays of 1979 (Shirley Gee: *Typhoid Mary;* Carey Harrison: *I Never Killed My German;* Barrie Keeffe: *Heaven Scent;* John Kirkmorris: *Coxcomb;* John Peacock: *Attard in Retirement;* Olwen Wymark: *The Child)*
	Best Radio Plays of 1980 (Stewart Parker: *The Kamikaze Ground Staff Reunion Dinner;* Martyn Read: *Waving to a Train;* Peter Redgrave: *Martyr of the Hives;* William Trevor: *Beyond the Pale)*